GERMANY

 **Marshall Cavendish**
Benchmark

New York

Written by: Nicole Frank and Richard Lord
Editors: Peter Mavrikis, Cheryl Sim
Publisher: Michelle Bisson
Series Designer: Benson Tan

Photo research by Thomas Khoo and Susan Jane Manuel

Originated and designed by Marshall Cavendish International (Asia) Pte Ltd
Copyright © 2011 Marshall Cavendish International (Asia) Pte Ltd
Published by Marshall Cavendish Benchmark
An imprint of Marshall Cavendish Corporation
All rights reserved.

This publication represents the opinions and views of the authors based on
Nicole Frank and Richard Lord's personal experience, knowledge, and research.
The information in this book serves as a general guide only. The authors and
publisher have used their best efforts in preparing this book and disclaim
liability rising directly and indirectly from the use and application of this book.

Other Marshall Cavendish Offices:
Marshall Cavendish International (Asia) Pte Ltd, 1 New Industrial Road,
Singapore 536196 ● Marshall Cavendish International (Thailand) Co Ltd.
253 Asoke, 12th Flr, Sukhumvit 21 Road, Klongtoey Nua, Wattana,
Bangkok 10110, Thailand ● Marshall Cavendish (Malaysia) Sdn Bhd,
Times Subang, Lot 46, Subang Hi-Tech Industrial Park, Batu Tiga,
40000 Shah Alam, Selangor Darul Ehsan, Malaysia

Marshall Cavendish is a trademark of Times Publishing Limited.
All websites were available and accurate when this book was sent to press.

Library of Congress Cataloging-in-Publication Data
Frank, Nicole.
Germany / Nicole Frank and Richard Lord.
p. cm. — (Welcome to my country)
Summary: "An overview of the history, geography, government, economy,
language, people, and culture of Germany. Includes numerous color photos,
useful facts, and a detailed map and resource section"
—Provided by publisher.
Includes index.
ISBN 978-1-60870-154-4
1. Germany—Juvenile literature. I. Lord, Richard A. (Richard Alan)
II. Title.
DD17.F725 2011
943—dc22   2010010514

Printed in Malaysia
135642

PHOTO CREDITS
Alamy: 3 (top), 11 (left), 17 (right), 21, 22, 23, 28, 38 (top)
Art Directors & TRIP Photo Library: 27
Axiom Photographic Agency: 1, 7, 35
Corbis: 8 (top), 11 (right), 15 (all), 30 (top), 34, 38 (bottom)
Dave G. Houser Stock Photography: 5, 40, 43, 45
Getty Images: 31, 37
Hutchison Library: 3 (center), 18
Inter Nationes: 3 (bottom), 10 (all), 13 (top), 17 (left), 29 (top),
    30 (bottom), 33
International Photobank: 26
Photolibrary: 4, 16, 19, 24 (both), 25, 29 (bottom), 32
Topham Picturepoint: cover, 2, 6, 8 (bottom), 9, 12, 13 (bottom), 14,
    20, 36 (both), 39, 41

Contents

Words that appear in the glossary are printed in **boldface** type the first time they occur in the text.

Many people visit the Marienplatz, a central square in Munich. The building on the right is the city hall.

Welcome to Germany!

Germany is famous for its contributions to world culture. The country was divided into East Germany and West Germany in 1949 and **reunified** in 1990. Join us on a tour of Germany and learn all about the German people!

Germans enjoy eating and relaxing at an outdoor café in Berlin.

The Flag of Germany

The current flag was used during many periods in German history. Both East and West Germany have used the same flag, but the East German flag included a **coat of arms** in the center featuring a hammer and compass. Reunified Germany kept the West German flag.

The Land

Covering an area of 137,846 square miles (357,022 square kilometers), Germany is the third largest country in the **European Union**, after France and Spain.

Germany has some of the world's most beautiful mountains and rivers. The Harz Mountains make up part of the landscape in central Germany, and the Bavarian Alps lie in southern

The Alps form the border between Germany and Austria. At 9,718 feet (2,962 meters), the highest peak in Germany is Zugspitze.

Hamburg is Germany's largest port. The Alster, Bille, and Elbe Rivers meet in this city, making it an important trading center.

Germany. Large rivers, such as the Rhine, Elbe, Danube, Weser, Oder, and Main, flow across the country.

Northern Germany consists of a broad, flat plain that reaches the North Sea.

Seasons

Germany has a temperate climate with four seasons. The southern Alps experience the coldest temperatures. The **sirocco**, a warm wind from Africa, gives southwestern Germany a mild, comfortable climate.

The Black Forest is a popular vacation destination.

Plants and Animals

Forests cover almost one-third of Germany. The dark fir trees of Baden-Württemberg give the famous Black Forest its name.

This house is surrounded by the spectacular beauty of the Bavarian landscape.

The osprey is among the rare bird species that nest in Germany's nature reserves.

Today, citizens and tourists hike the forest trails to look at the animals and enjoy the scenery.

Germany is home to many animals, including vultures, hawks, foxes, badgers, elk, and deer. Nature reserves protect much of the land along the former border between East and West Germany. These reserves provide a home for rare animals, such as lynx, wolves, bears, and sea eagles.

History

Not much is known about German history before 9 CE. In that year, Germanic tribes fought off the Roman army at the Rhine and Danube Rivers. For the next four centuries, the tribes lived alongside the Romans. When the Roman Empire collapsed in 476, a Germanic tribe called the Franks took power. By 700, they had conquered a large part of western Europe.

Charlemagne, known as Karl der Grosse in Germany, made Latin the official language of the Frankish Empire.

From Charlemagne to Bismarck

Charlemagne ruled the Franks from 768 to 814. He expanded the Frankish Empire. When he died, the empire was divided among his sons. Power struggles between rulers and with the Catholic Church continued for the next three hundred years.

In 1517, a German monk named Martin Luther posted his complaints about the Catholic Church on a church door. His action led to the **Reformation**, when the Roman Catholic Church split into the Protestant and Catholic denominations. The two groups

Martin Luther separated from the Catholic Church and helped create the Protestant **denomination**.

(**Left**) Otto von Bismarck was the prime minister of Prussia. He helped create and lead the successful German Empire. (**Right**) King William I of Prussia was the first kaiser (KYE-zer), or emperor, of the German Empire. Formed on January 18, 1871, the empire lasted forty-seven years.

struggled for power throughout the sixteenth century. The Thirty Years' War (1618–1648) left Germany further divided into many small kingdoms under different rulers.

In 1871, Otto von Bismarck, the prime minister of Prussia (the largest German state) reunified the German kingdoms. Bismarck helped create the German Empire, or *Reich* (RIKE).

Under Hitler's rule, numerous **concentration camps** were built and used to contain and kill Jewish people and other select groups considered to be enemies of Nazi Germany.

War and Division

As Germany's power grew, conflicts with other countries arose. From 1914 to 1918, Germany fought World War I against many other nations. The Reich ended with Germany's defeat. A new government was set up, but Adolf Hitler and his National Socialist Party, or the Nazis, seized power in 1933.

Led by Hitler, Germany invaded Poland and, in 1939, Great Britain and France declared war on Germany. The United States entered the war against Germany in 1941.

On May 8, 1945, Germany surrendered, and the Nazi government collapsed.

After World War II, four countries occupied Germany. In 1949, the zones held by the United States, Great Britain, and France formed democratic West Germany. The zone controlled by the Soviet Union became **Communist** East Germany.

The Berlin Airlift memorial was built to honor people who flew supplies into Berlin in 1948, after the Soviet Union sealed off all land routes to the city.

In 1961, East Germany built the Berlin Wall to keep East Germans from escaping to West Germany. The border between the two countries became known as the Iron Curtain.

The Road to Reunification

After World War II, both East and West German economies prospered, but conflicts continued between the two countries. From 1961 to 1989, the Berlin Wall kept the two Germanys divided. In 1989, however, Communism collapsed in Europe. The Berlin Wall came down, and Germany reunified on October 3, 1990, amidst much celebration.

On October 3, 1990, Germans celebrated their country's reunification at the parliament building in Berlin.

Louis II (1845—1886)

German-born Louis II was king of Bavaria from 1864 to 1886. He urged Germany's princes to form an empire. In his later years, he withdrew from politics to focus on the arts. Often called "Mad King Ludwig," he was declared insane and **deposed** in 1886.

Louis II

Adolf Hitler (1889—1945)

Austrian-born Adolf Hitler was the leader of the National Socialist (Nazi) Party. In 1933, he became **chancellor** of Germany. His policies led to World War II and caused much suffering.

Adolf Hitler

Konrad Adenauer (1876—1967)

Konrad Adenauer began his political career in 1906. Under the Nazis, he was sent to a concentration camp. He reentered politics after the war, becoming the first chancellor of West Germany in 1949.

Konrad Adenauer

The Government and the Economy

Germany is a democratic republic with two houses of parliament—the **Bundestag** (boon-des-TAHG), consisting of elected representatives, and the **Bundesrat** (boon-des-RAHT), made up of appointed lawmakers. Germany has sixteen states, each with its own elected parliament.

The Reichstag Building in Berlin is the official meeting place of Germany's government and is also a major tourist attraction where visitors flock to its famous glass-domed roof terrace.

(**Left**) Helmut Kohl became the first chancellor of reunified Germany in 1990.
(**Right**) Angela Merkel was appointed chancellor in 2005. She is also the country's first woman to hold the nation's highest office.

Leading Germany

All German citizens over the age of eighteen have the right to vote. The main political parties in Germany include the Christian Democratic Union (CDU), the Social Democratic Party (SDP), and the Green Party.

As the head of the Bundestag's majority party, the chancellor is the most powerful person in Germany. Parliament elects the president, whose role is largely **ceremonial**.

German **industrialization** began in the early 1800s in the Ruhr Valley. Today, more than a third of Germany's labor force is involved in manufacturing.

A Thriving Economy

Since the 1960s, Germany has been Europe's largest economy, and has consistently ranked among the four largest economies in the world. It exports electronics, cars, and food to countries all over the world. The German currency, formerly the Deutsche mark, is now the Euro.

Transportation

Germany's transportation system is extremely modern and efficient. Frankfurt International Airport is the country's busiest airport and is connected to the most international destinations in the world. There are numerous ports and harbors, as well as a network of railroads and subways. The **Autobahn** (AW-to-bahn), Germany's system of highways, is world famous.

On the Job

Germans work hard and enjoy about six weeks of paid vacation a year. Labor unions guard the welfare of employees.

Germany's rivers have always been important for trade. River cruises are a fun way to sightsee!

People and Lifestyle

About 82 million people live in Germany. Most of their ancestors came from other parts of western Europe.

Germans are proud of the regions in which they were born. Their overall German identity often comes second, after their identity as Bavarians, Saxons, Swabians, Hessians, or East Friesians.

These young children are wearing the regional dress of Bavaria. Traditional outfits are now used mainly for special occasions.

Turks, Italians, Greeks, Spaniards, Moroccans, and citizens of the former Yugoslavia make up the largest groups of foreigners in Germany.

Today, most Germans live in cities and towns. Many make their homes in modern apartment buildings. Since reunification, thousands of East Germans moved to the major cities in the western part of the country.

About 15 million immigrants live in Germany. Many originally came from other European countries and from Asia. The city of Frankfurt has the largest immigrant population.

Family Life

German families rarely have more than two children. Larger households are more common in the countryside than in the cities. Both parents usually work to support the family.

Germans love traveling. Many families take short vacations abroad during the summer months and school holidays.

Dogs and other house pets are treated like members of the family in Germany.

Holidays such as Christmas are a time for families to be together. This family enjoys skating on a rink in a Christmas market in Hamburg.

Education

All students attend school together until the fifth grade, when they are tested and divided according to the results. The *Hauptschule* (HOWPT-shool-uh) trains pupils for jobs in trade and industry. The *Realschule* (ray-AHL-shool-uh) prepares them for mid-level jobs. The *Gymnasium* (gim-NAH-zee-oom) prepares them for a university and executive-level jobs.

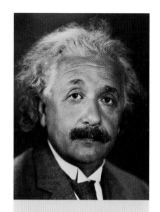

Germany is a highly educated country that has produced many great scientists and researchers. Albert Einstein received the Nobel Prize in Physics in 1921.

Lessons are conducted in German. Many pupils study English as a second language.

Students take the bus home after school. All German children must attend school for at least nine years. Gymnasium students go to school for thirteen years.

The school day lasts from early morning until noon in Germany. Schools do not have sports teams or other activities, so students pursue their leisure interests by joining clubs and other community organizations.

Each state runs its own schools. About 5 percent of children attend private schools. About 25 percent of students attend a university. Students help decide how the university is run.

Religion

Freedom of religion is protected in Germany. About 28 million people are members of the Lutheran Church, and close to 30 million belong to the Roman Catholic Church. Despite their large numbers, only 5 percent of Lutherans

Artist Marc Chagall designed the colorful stained glass windows of St. Stephen's Church in Mainz.

More than 4 million Muslims, mostly Turkish immigrants, live in Germany.

and 19 percent of Catholics in Germany go to church regularly. Public schools offer religious classes. Church members also pay a tax to the government to help support the work of the Church.

Islam is Germany's largest minority religion. Other religious faiths in Germany are Judaism, Methodist, and Baptist.

Language

Did you know that English began as a German **dialect** and developed into a separate language over time? This is why, even now, the German and English languages share many similarities.

Pronouncing German words is not hard once you know the main differences between German and English—Germans pronounce the letter "W" like the English "V" and pronounce the letter "V" like the English "F."

German and English belong to the same family of languages.

Literature

German literature began with the ancient myths and legends of German gods and heroes. During the 1400s, Martin Luther translated the Bible into German. The invention of the printing press around 1440 popularized the German language. In the eighteenth century, German author Johann Wolfgang von Goethe wrote *Faust*, the story of a man who sells his soul to the devil in return for all the knowledge in the world.

Other famous German writers include Thomas Mann, Bertolt Brecht, Herman Hesse, Günter Grass, and Heinrich Böll.

Günter Grass wrote many works about the hardships Germans faced during World War II.

The Brothers Grimm wrote a collection of fairy tales in the 1800s which included "Hansel and Gretel." These short stories are still enjoyed by children today.

Arts

Germany has made many contributions to the arts, and Germans describe themselves as a *kulturvolk* (kool-TOOR-fulk), or "a people of culture."

You may be familiar with some of Germany's great composers. You may even have played music written by Bach, Brahms, Handel, Beethoven, or Schumann.

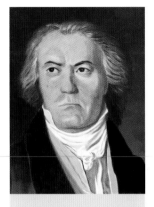

The works of classical composer Ludwig van Beethoven (1770–1827) are famous throughout the world.

German children are encouraged to study music. Today, there are about two hundred orchestras in Germany.

Self portrait of German painter Hans Holbein the Younger (1497—1543).

Painting and Sculpture

Early German art focused mainly on religious themes. The late 1400s and the 1500s produced renowned artists, such as Albrecht Dürer and Hans Holbein the Younger. Art in the seventeenth century was stalled by the Thirty Years' War. **Baroque** arrived in the eighteenth century, while neoclassical and Romantic styles flourished in the nineteenth century. The pain and loss of both world wars were common twentieth-century themes. Today, Germany has more than 1,500 museums and art galleries. Works of art are also displayed in public spaces.

Architecture and Theater

The earliest examples of German architecture were the cathedrals of the ninth century. From the mid-1600s, beautiful castles were built in the baroque style in Germany.

From the 1920s, architects brought simple designs to ordinary buildings, such as factories and offices.

After World War II, cities had to be rebuilt as quickly as possible. Therefore, German architects emphasized plainness and **function** rather than style.

Architect Walter Gropius designed the Bauhaus Modern Art College, with its simple lines. Gropius favored designs for ordinary people, not for the rich.

Movie star Marlene Dietrich moved to Hollywood during the 1930s after the Nazis took control of Germany.

In the 1920s, Berlin theater reached a high point with the work of poet/playwright Bertolt Brecht and director Max Reinhardt. However, many artists left Germany when the Nazis took power. Today, the performing arts scene is thriving in Germany with hundreds of theaters across the country regularly staging operas, musicals, plays, and dance productions.

Leisure Time

People of all ages join clubs, called *vereine* (fur-INE-hun), in Germany. With more than 300,000 registered clubs in the country, there is a club for just about anything—bike riding, stamp collecting, dog breeding, and more! Since German schools do not offer recreational activities, sports clubs are extremely popular. One-third of all Germans belong to a sports club.

Hammersbach, a town in the state of Hesse, even has a Maypole Club! In May 2009, members of the club put up Germany's highest maypole on Zugspitze.

Members of a soccer club pose for a picture after a game.

The Beautiful Outdoors

Germany's forests and mountains attract many hikers. Rock climbing and skiing are other favorite activities.

Top of Their Game

Soccer, or *fussball* (FOOS-ball), is Germany's most popular sport. The West German team won the World Cup in 1954, 1974, and 1990. The women's soccer team has won twice, in 2003 and 2007.

Famous German athletes include figure skater Katarina Witt, Tour de France winner Jan Ulrich, tennis players Boris Becker and Steffi Graf, as well as Formula One driver Michael

(**Left**) At the age of seventeen, Boris Becker won the Wimbledon singles title. (**Right**) Steffi Graf was at the top of women's tennis for ten years.

Formula One racecar driver Michael Schumacher has won the F1 World Championship seven times, making him the driver with the most Grand Prix wins in Formula One history.

Schumacher. All of them have achieved international success in their sports. Britta Steffen is one of Germany's most promising young athletes. The swimming star won two gold medals at the 2008 Olympics, and she also holds three world records in freestyle swimming.

Festivals

Germany celebrates its biggest festival, Karneval (KAHR-neh-vahl), or Carnival, in February. Karneval marks the beginning of Lent, the forty-day period of fasting before Easter.

German festivals attract both locals and tourists. Many celebrations center around farming events. Munich's Oktoberfest is a

Karneval participants wear colorful masks and costumes.

The bright lights of Oktoberfest illuminate the city of Munich.

Traditional dancers perform at a festival in southern Germany.

huge beer festival held every October. In November, the
Rhineland celebrates its grape harvest.

Christmas festivities begin well before December 25.
In the cities, street markets inspire people to get into the
Christmas spirit. On Christmas Eve, families gather for a
big celebration.

Food

Germans love good food. The main meal is served in the middle of the day. Dinner tends to be a lighter meal, consisting of bread, cold cuts, cheese, and salad.

In the late afternoon, people eat rolls and cakes with coffee or tea. Children enjoy hot chocolate or fruit juice instead of coffee.

Pretzels are a favorite German food and come in many different varieties, including salty, sweet, and plain.

Did you know that hot dogs, or frankfurters, originally came from the city of Frankfurt?

Delicious Dishes

Favorite German foods include potatoes, sauerkraut (a pickled cabbage), and apple strudel (a dessert made with apples, raisins, and ground almonds). *Schnitzel* (SHNIT-tsuhl) is a breaded pork cutlet. German *wurst* (VORST), or sausage, is made with pork and other meats.

As the Germans say, "*Guten appetit*" (GOO-ten upp-eh-TEET), or "Enjoy your meal!"

GERMANY

SWEDEN

DENMARK

N

BALTIC SEA

NORTH SEA

Kiel

SCHLESWIG-
HOLSTEIN

Hamburg

MECKLENBURG-
WESTERN POMERANIA

POLAND

Bremen

Weser

Elbe

Oder

THE NETHERLANDS

LOWER SAXONY

Hannover

Hameln

Magdeburg

BERLIN

BRANDENBURG

Wittenberg

NORTH
RHINE-WESTPHALIA

HARZ MTS

SAXONY-ANHALT

Saale

Dortmund

*Ruhr
Industrial
Area*

Düsseldorf

Leipzig

Elbe

SAXONY

Cologne

Bonn

THURINGIA

Dresden

BELGIUM

Rhine

RHINELAND-
PALATINATE

TAUNUS MTS.

HESSE

Frankfurt

Hanau

Main

Mainz

Mannheim

SAARLAND

Heidelberg

Nuremberg
(Nürnberg)

BAVARIA

Bavarian Forest

CZECH
REPUBLIC

LUXEMBOURG

FRANCE

Karlsruhe

Rhine

Black Forest

Stuttgart

Tübingen

Danube

BADEN-
WÜRTTEMBERG

Munich

Oberammergau

BERCHTESGADEN ALPS

AUSTRIA

BAVARIAN ALPS

*Zugspitze
(9,718 feet/2,962 meters)*

SWITZERLAND

ITALY

———	International Boundary
———	State Boundary
■	Capital
●	City
▲	Mountain Peak
~~	River

A B C D

1

2

3

4

5

Street musicians play for passersby in a plaza in Frankfurt.

Austria D5

Baden-Württemberg
    B4
Baltic Sea D1
Bavaria C4
Bavarian Alps C5
Bavarian Forest
    C4–D4
Belgium A3
Berchtesgaden Alps C5
Berlin C2
Black Forest B4–B5
Bonn A3
Brandenburg C2–D2
Bremen B2

Cologne A3
Czech Republic
    D3–D4

Danube C4
Denmark B1–C1
Dortmund B3
Düsseldorf A3
Dresden D3

Elbe River C2–C3

France A4
Frankfurt B3

Hamburg B2
Hamein B2
Hanau B3
Hannover B2
Harz Mountains C3
Heidelberg B4
Hesse B3

Italy C5

Karlsruhe B4
Kiel B1

Leipzig C3
Lower Saxony B2
Luxembourg A4

Magdeburg C2
Main River C3
Mainz B4
Mecklenburg-Western
    Pomerania C2
Munich C4

Netherlands A2

North Rhine-
    Westphalia B2–B3
Nuremberg C4

Oberammergau C5
Oder River D2

Poland D2

Rhine River B3–B4
Rhineland-Palatinate
    A3–B3
Ruhr Industrial
    Area A3

Saale C3
Saarland A4

Saxony C3–D3
Saxony-Anhalt C3
Schleswig-Holstein
    B1–B2
Stuttgart B4
Sweden C1–D1
Switzerland B5

Taunus Mountains
    B3
Thuringia C3
Tübingen B4

Weser River B2
Wittenberg C3

Zugspitze C5

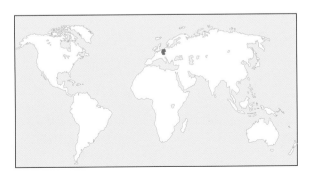

Quick Facts

Official Name Federal Republic of Germany

Capital Berlin

Official Language German

Population 82,329,758 (July 2009 estimate)

Land Area 137,846 square miles (357,022 square kilometers)

Provinces Baden–Württemberg, Bavaria, Berlin, Brandenburg, Bremen, Hamburg, Hesse, Lower Saxony, Meckleburg–Western Pomerania, North Rhine–Westphalia, Rhineland–Palatinate, Saarland, Saxony, Saxony–Anhalt, Schleswig–Holstein, Thuringia

Highest Point Zugspitze, 9,718 feet (2,962 meters)

Major Rivers Elbe, Main, Rhine

Major Mountains Bavarian Alps, Harz Mountains

Major Festivals Karneval (February), Oktoberfest (October), Christmas (December 25)

National Anthem *Das Deutschlandlied* ("Song of Germany")

Currency Euro (0.72 EUR = U.S. $1 in 2010)

Berlin's Charlottenburg Palace was once the summer home of Prussian kings.

Glossary

Autobahn: A network of highways stretching over 6,835 miles (11,000 kilometers) in Germany.

baroque: A style in architecture and art of the early seventeenth to mid-eighteenth century. The baroque style is marked by ornate patterns that suggest movement.

Bundesrat: The house of appointed lawmakers in the German parliament.

Bundestag: The house in the German parliament consisting of 672 elected representatives.

ceremonial: Relating to formal requirements rather than having political authority.

chancellor: The leader of the German government.

coat of arms: A design or symbolic emblem.

Communist: Relating to a political movement based on the ideas of German philosopher Karl Marx. Under Communism, all property belongs to the community or state.

concentration camp: A guarded compound for the confinement of political prisoners. An estimated 6 million people, many of them Jews, died in Nazi concentration camps during World War II.

denomination: A religious organization that unites numerous congregations.

deposed: Removed from power.

dialect: A regional variety of a certain language.

European Union: A group of European countries that promotes free trade.

function: A certain type of duty.

Gymnasium: A school that prepares students for university studies and executive positions in industry and commerce.

Hauptschule: A school that prepares students for jobs in trade and industry.

industrialization: The act of building factories and introducing manufacturing on a large scale.

Realschule: A school that prepares students for mid-level jobs in business and public service.

Reformation: The sixteenth-century movement for change in the Roman Catholic Church.

reunified: Joined together again.

sirocco: A warm wind from Africa.

For More Information

Books

Alcraft, Rob. *A Visit to Germany*. Portsmouth, NH: Heinemann Library, 2008.

Byers, Ann. *Germany: A Primary Source Culture Guide*. New York: PowerPlus Books, 2005.

Flint, David. *Focus on Germany*. Strongsville, OH: Gareth Stevens Publishing, 2006.

Russell, Henry. *National Geographic Countries of the World: Germany*. Des Moines, IA: National Geographic Children's Books, 2007.

Salas, Laura Purdie. *Germany*. Mankato, MN: Capstone Press, 2006.

Salzman, Amanda. *Mike's Adventure Packs: Germany*. Winfield, KS: Salzman Books, LLC, 2009.

DVDs

Discovering Germany. (Educational Video Network, Inc., 2006).

Germany: A Musical Tour of Bach's Homeland. (Naxos DVD, 2008).

Visions of Germany. (Acorn Media, 2007).

Websites

www.aupairinamerica.com/resources/kids/culture_corner/germany.asp

A site with fun activities to do, that include learning simple German, and whipping up treats like *marmokuchen* (marble cake) and apple strudel.

www.europe-cities.com/en/630/germany/

A detailed guide showcasing key facts about Germany, such as history and culture, as well as sightseeing suggestions.

www.germany.info/Vertretung/usa/en/09__Videos__Fun/04__Kids/00__Kids.html

A delightful portal with easy-to-read snippets, written for children by the German Missions in the United States.

www.grimmfairytales.com/en/main

Features a compilation of popular tales written by the Brothers Grimm.

Index